First World War
and Army of Occupation
War Diary
France, Belgium and Germany

GUARDS DIVISION
1 Guards Brigade
Coldstream Guards
3 Battalion
1 August 1915 -1 February 1919

WO95/1215/3-4

The Naval & Military Press Ltd
www.nmarchive.com
Published in association with The National Archives

Published by

The Naval & Military Press Ltd

Unit 10 Ridgewood Industrial Park,

Uckfield, East Sussex,

TN22 5QE England

Tel: +44 (0) 1825 749494

www.naval-military-press.com

www.nmarchive.com

This diary has been reprinted in facsimile from the original. Any imperfections are inevitably reproduced and the quality may fall short of modern type and cartographic standards.

© Crown Copyright
Images reproduced by permission of The National Archives, London, England, 2015.

Contents

Document type	Place/Title	Date From	Date To
Heading	1915 Aug-1919 2nd Batt Grenadier Guards		
Heading	B E F Guards Div 1 Guards Bde 3 Coldstream G.D.S 1918 Aug-1918 Jan And Nov 1918-1919 Feb		
Heading	1st Guards Brigade. Guards Division War Diary 3rd Battn. Coldstream Guards August 1915		
Miscellaneous	On His Majesty's Service.		
War Diary		01/08/1915	31/08/1915
Heading	War Diary 3rd Battn. Coldstream Guards September 1915		
Miscellaneous	On His Majesty's Service.		
Heading	Guards Division 3rd Bn. Coldstream Gds Sep 1915 Vol X		
War Diary		01/09/1915	30/09/1915
Heading	1st Guards Brigade Guards Division War Diary 3rd Battn. Coldstream Guards October 1915		
Miscellaneous	On His Majesty's Service.		
War Diary		01/10/1915	31/10/1915
Heading	1st Guards Brigade. Guards Division War Diary 3rd Battn. Coldstream Guards November 1915		
Miscellaneous	On His Majesty's Service.		
War Diary		01/11/1915	30/11/1915
Heading	1st Guards Brigade. Guards Division War Diary 3rd Battn. Coldstream Guards December 1915		
Miscellaneous	On His Majesty's Service.		
War Diary		01/12/1915	31/12/1915
Heading	1st Guards Brigade. Guards Division. 3rd Battalion Coldstream Guards. January 1916		
War Diary		01/01/1916	31/01/1916
Heading	1st Guards Brigade. Guards Division 3rd Battalion Coldstream Guards February 1916		
War Diary		01/02/1916	29/02/1916
Heading	1st Guards Brigade. Guards Division 3rd Battalion Coldstream Guards March 1916		
Heading	3 Coldstream Gd Vol XIV		
War Diary		01/03/1916	31/03/1916
Heading	1st Guards Brigade. Guards Division 3rd Battalion Coldstream Guards April 1916		
War Diary		01/04/1916	30/04/1916
Heading	1st Guards Brigade. Guards Division 3rd Battalion Coldstream Guards May 1916		
War Diary		01/05/1916	31/05/1916
Heading	1st Guards Brigade. Guards Division. 3rd Battalion Coldstream Guards June 1916		
War Diary		01/06/1916	30/06/1916
Heading	1st Guards Brigade. Guards Division 3rd Battalion Coldstream Guards July 1916		
War Diary		01/07/1916	31/07/1916
Heading	1st Guards Brigade. Guards Division 3rd Battalion Coldstream Guards August 1916		
War Diary		01/08/1916	31/08/1916

Heading	1st Brigade. Guards Division 3rd Battalion Coldstream Guards September 1916		
War Diary		01/09/1916	30/09/1916
Heading	1st Guards Brigade. Guards Division 3rd Battalion Coldstream Guards October 1916		
War Diary		01/10/1916	31/10/1916
Heading	1st Guards Brigade. Guards Division 3rd Battalion Coldstream Guards November 1916		
War Diary	Selincourt	01/11/1916	30/11/1916
Heading	1st Guards Brigade. Guards Division 3rd Battalion Coldstream Guards December 1916		
War Diary	Forked Tree Camp	01/12/1916	02/12/1916
War Diary	Maltz. Horn	03/12/1916	05/12/1916
War Diary	Trenches	05/12/1916	05/12/1916
War Diary	Malzhorn	06/12/1916	06/12/1916
War Diary	Bromfay	07/12/1916	09/12/1916
War Diary	Combles	10/12/1916	10/12/1916
War Diary	Trenches	11/12/1916	12/12/1916
War Diary	Malzhorn	13/12/1916	13/12/1916
War Diary	Baumeny	14/12/1916	15/12/1916
War Diary	Combles	16/12/1916	16/12/1916
War Diary	Trenches	17/12/1916	18/12/1916
War Diary	Bronfay	19/12/1916	21/12/1916
War Diary	Combles	22/12/1916	22/12/1916
War Diary	Trenches	22/12/1916	24/12/1916
War Diary	Bronfay	25/12/1916	27/12/1916
War Diary	Combles	28/12/1916	28/12/1916
War Diary	Trenches	29/12/1916	30/12/1916
War Diary	Bronfay	31/12/1916	31/12/1916
War Diary	Meaulte	01/01/1917	24/01/1917
War Diary	Billon Wood	25/01/1917	28/01/1917
War Diary	Priez Farm	29/01/1917	31/01/1917
War Diary	Priez Fm	01/02/1917	02/02/1917
War Diary	Billon 107	03/02/1917	09/02/1917
War Diary	Maurepas Ravine	10/02/1917	10/02/1917
War Diary	Trenches	10/02/1917	14/02/1917
War Diary	Maurepas Ravine	14/02/1917	18/02/1917
War Diary	Trenches	18/02/1917	22/02/1917
War Diary	Maurepas Ravine	22/02/1917	25/02/1917
War Diary	Billon Camp	25/02/1917	28/02/1917
War Diary	Billon	01/03/1917	12/03/1917
War Diary	Fregicourt	13/03/1917	15/03/1917
War Diary	Trenches	16/03/1917	17/03/1917
War Diary	Fregicourt	18/03/1917	19/03/1917
War Diary	Maurepas	20/03/1917	22/03/1917
War Diary	Montauban	23/03/1917	30/04/1917
War Diary	Bronfay Camp 16	01/05/1917	07/05/1917
War Diary	Le Transloy	08/05/1917	10/05/1917
War Diary	Rocquiny	11/05/1917	19/05/1917
War Diary	Bronfay Camp 15	20/05/1917	20/05/1917
War Diary	Vaux	21/05/1917	31/05/1917
War Diary	Clairmarais	01/06/1917	30/06/1917
War Diary	Trenches Boesinghe	01/07/1917	02/07/1917
War Diary	Cardoen Fm	03/07/1917	07/07/1917
War Diary	Trenches X Line Boesinghe Sector	08/07/1917	11/07/1917
War Diary	Roussel Fm	12/07/1917	14/07/1917

War Diary	Proven	15/07/1917	15/07/1917
War Diary	Herzeele	16/07/1917	24/07/1917
War Diary	A 4 C	25/07/1917	26/07/1917
War Diary	Trenches Boesinghe Sector	27/07/1917	27/07/1917
War Diary	Trenches	28/07/1917	29/07/1917
War Diary	Forest Area	30/07/1917	30/07/1917
War Diary	Trenches	31/07/1917	04/08/1917
War Diary	Paddock Wood Camp	05/08/1917	31/08/1917
War Diary	Charterhouse Camp	01/09/1917	08/09/1917
War Diary	Trenches	08/09/1917	12/09/1917
War Diary	Henley Camp	13/09/1917	20/09/1917
War Diary	Paddock Wood	20/09/1917	31/10/1917
Miscellaneous	Narrative of Operations From Nov 27th 6pm To Dec 5th		
War Diary	Nortleulinghem	01/11/1917	30/11/1917
War Diary		01/12/1917	31/12/1917
Heading	3rd Coldstream Gds January 1918		
War Diary	Berneville	01/01/1918	02/01/1918
War Diary	Arras	02/01/1918	10/01/1918
War Diary	Pudding Trench	10/01/1918	14/01/1918
War Diary	Trenches	14/01/1918	26/01/1918
War Diary	Arras	26/01/1918	31/01/1918

BEF

Guards Div.

1 Guards Bde

3 Coldstream Gds

1 DG   1917 Jan
AND
1/6 1918   1919 Feb

1917 to Apr 1918

FROM 2 DIV 4 Bde

1st Guards Brigade.
Guards Division.

3rd BATTN. COLDSTREAM GUARDS.

A U G U S T

1 9 1 5

On His Majesty's Service.

WAR DIARY or **INTELLIGENCE SUMMARY.**
(Erase heading not required.)

Army Form C. 2118.

3rd Batt. Coldstream Gds

Hour, Date, Place	Summary of Events and Information	Remarks and references to Appendices
Aug 14th to 14th	In bivouac GIVENCHY	
15th	Relieved in the trenches by 2nd Batt. H.L.I. Moved into billets BETHUNE	
16th — 18th	In billets at BETHUNE	
19th	Brigade marched out of BETHUNE to FONTES	
20th		
21st	Marched from FONTES to ARQUES	
22nd & 23rd	Marched from ARQUES via STOMER to GANSPETTE	
	In billets at GANSPETTE	
24th	Marched from GANSPETTE via WIZERNES to CLETY	
25th — 31st	In billets at CLETY	

M.V. Crawford Lieut
3rd Batt Colds Guards

1st Guards Brigade.
Guards Division.

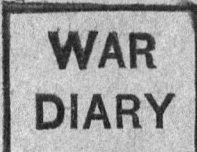

3rd BATTN. COLDSTREAM GUARDS.

SEPTEMBER

1915

On His Majesty's Service.

(G.Bn

121/7530

Guards 5 Wrenn

3rd Bn. Coldstream Gds.

S.15.

I G-Bdes-

Vol X

In Loos fighting 27/9/15 - not much fighting
repulsed a German counter attack 8/10/15
but they don't say N exactly where
very vague, evidently somewhere
near Vermelles

WAR DIARY
or
INTELLIGENCE SUMMARY

Army Form C. 2118.

3rd Batt'n Coldstream Guards

Hour, Date, Place	Summary of Events and Information	Remarks and references to Appendices
Sept 1st	In Billets at CLETY. Brigade Field Day	
2nd	Marched from CLETY to MAVRANS.	
3rd, 21st	In billets at MAVRANS.	
22nd	Marched from MAVRANS to MAISNIL.	
23rd	Marched from MAISNIL to WESTREHEM.	
24th	In billets at WESTREHEM.	
25th	Marched from WESTREHEM (via AUCHEL) to NOEUX-les-Mines	
26th	Marched from NOEUX les MINES to SAILLY-LA-BOURSE to VERMELLES. Then took up the extended line of trenches	
	north of VERMELLES – HULLUCH road. The whole	
	formed into the Guards Pont Guard.	
27th	Moved forward to a line of trenches S. of Hulluch	
	from G. Bn to A.I.	
28th – 30th	In trenches just South East of HULLUCH.	

1st Guards Brigade.
Guards Division.

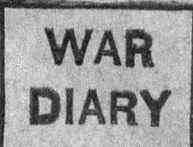

3rd BATTN. COLDSTREAM GUARDS.

OCTOBER

1915

On His Majesty's Service.

WAR DIARY or INTELLIGENCE SUMMARY.

Army Form C. 2118.

(Erase heading not required.)

Instructions regarding War Diaries and Intelligence Summaries are contained in F.S. Regs., Part II. and the Staff Manual respectively. Title pages will be prepared in manuscript.

5 + A.M. Brigade ...

Hour, Date, Place	Summary of Events and Information	Remarks and references to Appendices
Oct. 1st	Relieved in early morning by 7/8th Royal Scots Regt. marched to billets MAZINGARBE	
2nd	in billets at MAZINGARBE	
3rd	Relieved 1st Kings (Liverpool Regt) in trenches "OM" germans line N. of HULLOCH - VERMELLES road.	
4th	in trenches	
5th	Relieved by 2 G.G. and went to support line in old German trench	
6th	in support	
7th	Relieved 2 G.G. in front line	
8th	in trenches. Attack by 12th Div. in front of us at 12.15 pm to 3.10 pm. Counter attack by Germans – broken up easily	1 offr + 23 men wounded 1 offr + 65 men wounded
9th	retreat	
	Relieved by 10th Gloucester Regt. & 8th N. Staffs. marched to billets in MAZINGARBE	
10th - 11th	in reserve billets VERMELLES	
12th	marched to billets at VERQUIN	
13th	marched to billets at HESDIGNEUL	

Army Form C. 2118.

WAR DIARY
or
INTELLIGENCE SUMMARY.

(Erase heading not required.)

3rd Batt'n [illegible]

Hour, Date, Place	Summary of Events and Information	Remarks and references to Appendices
Aug 14	In billets at HESDIGNEUL.	
15	Marched from HESDIGNEUL to billets at BEUVRY-VERMELLES	
16		
17	In same billets at VERMELLES	
18	Relieved by 2 Q.C. marched to billets at SAILLY-LA-BOURSE	
19	In billets at SAILLY-LA-BOURSE	
20	Relieved 2 C.G. in the trenches	
21	In the trenches	
22		
23	Relieved by 2 C.G. [illegible] in VERMELLES	
24	In billets [illegible] VERMELLES	
25		
26	[illegible] 7th Bath supplied [illegible]	
27	HESDIGNEUL [illegible] at HESDIGNEUL	

Instructions regarding War Diaries and Intelligence
Summaries are contained in F. S. Regs., Part II.
and the Staff Manual respectively. Title pages
will be prepared in manuscript.

1st Guards Brigade.
Guards Division.

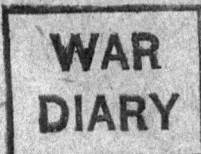

3rd BATTN. COLDSTREAM GUARDS.

NOVEMBER

1915

On His Majesty's Service.

Army Form C. 2118.

WAR DIARY
or
INTELLIGENCE SUMMARY.
(Erase heading not required.)

2nd Bn Coldstream Guards

Instructions regarding War Diaries and Intelligence Summaries are contained in F.S. Regs., Part II. and the Staff Manual respectively. Title pages will be prepared in manuscript.

Hour, Date, Place	Summary of Events and Information	Remarks and references to Appendices
Nov 1st to 9th.	Bn in Billets at HESDIGNEUL.	
10th	Marched to PARADIS	
11th 12th & 13th	In billets at PARADIS	
14th	Marched & billets at LA GORGUE	
14th to 20th	In billets at LA GORGUE	
20th	Battalion relieved 2nd Scots Guards in the trenches left sector of 1st Guards Brigade from M.29. d. 6.0. to M.30.a.0.7 (ref Trench Map 36 S N I/10,000)	
21st	Relieved by 2nd Bn Coldstream Guards at 4.30 A.M. Battalion went to billets at VIELLE CHAPELLE	
22nd 23rd	In billets at VIELLE CHAPELLE	
24th	Relieved 2nd Bn in Trenches – rain fell continued line to N.E. 900 yards & occupied as far as 59TH ST. Dispositions – 3 coys in front line & in support. TRUFFOY NORTH, GRANTS, DREADNOUGHT, ERITH, WINCHESTER	
25th	Lay holding portions of front. Relieved by 2nd Bn Coldstream Guards at at 3.0. Batt'n moved to billets at PONT DU HEM	
26th	In billets at PONT DU HEM	
27th	Relieved 2nd Bn Coldstream Guards in the trenches. Same dispositions.	
28th	In trenches. Very cold hard frost	
29th	Quick change in weather. Heavy rain. Trenches much damaged in consequence. Relieved by 2 C.G. 8.0 P.M. Battalion moved to billets at PONT DU HEM	
30th	In billets at PONT DU HEM	

J. Campbell
Lieut Colonel
Commanding
2nd Bn Coldstream Guards

1st Guards Brigade.
Guards Division.

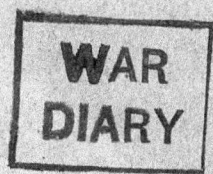

3rd BATTN. COLDSTREAM GUARDS.

DECEMBER

1915

On His Majesty's Service.

WAR DIARY or INTELLIGENCE SUMMARY

Army Form C. 2118.

3rd Bn Coldstream Guards

Hour, Date, Place	Summary of Events and Information	Remarks and references to Appendices
Dec. 1st 2nd	Relieved 2 C.G. in trenches 50 km. Rain throughout the day. Dugouts much damaged thereby. Battalion relieved at 6 to by 2nd Scots Guards (3rd Guards Bde) on relief, the Battn. moved back to billets at LA GORGUE.	
3rd to 8th	In billets at LA GORGUE.	
8th	1st Grenr. Bde. relieved 2nd Grenr. Bde. in the trenches. Relieved 2nd Bn Grenadier Guards at 51 km Gate. Relieved by daylight owing to communication (chief approach by daylight) trenches being full of water. 1st Battalion trenches and in of Bde.) from M.24 d. 2. 6½. to N. 13 d. 3. Supported: 4 Coys on the line. Very wet day & night.	Ref Trench Map 36 SW No. 000
9th 10th	In trenches. Heavy work on refront throughout day. Relieved by 2.C.G. Battalion moved to billets at LAVENTIE at 5 OP m.	
11th	In billets.	
12th	Relieved 2 C.G. in trenches 50 km - Same line.	
13th	In trenches. Situation normal. Work heavy.	
14th	Relieved by 2 C.G. at 5 Okm. (Moved to billets at LAVENTIE)	
15th	In billets.	
16th	Relieved 2 C.G. in trenches at 5 Okm.	
17th	In trenches. Weather very wet.	
18th	Situation normal. Very heavy fog 7am thick, thinned away. Relieved by 2.C.G. at 4.0 p.m. Cde settled in night of billets in LAVENTIE. Battalion moved to billets in LAVENTIE.	
19th	In billets.	

J. Campbell
Lieut. Colonel.
Comdg. 3rd Bn Coldstream Guards

Army Form C. 2118.

WAR DIARY
or
INTELLIGENCE SUMMARY.

(Erase heading not required.)

3rd Battn. Coldstream Guards

Instructions regarding War Diaries and Intelligence Summaries are contained in F.S. Regs., Part II. and the Staff Manual respectively. Title pages will be prepared in manuscript.

Hour, Date, Place	Summary of Events and Information	Remarks and references to Appendices
Dec 20th	1st Guards Bde relieved by 3rd Guards Bde Battn. marched back to billets near MERVILLE.	
20th-26th	In billets at MERVILLE.	
26th	1st Guards Bde relieved 2nd Guards Bde in trenches. Battn. marched up to billets at PONT DU HEM.	
27th	Relieved 2 C.G. in trenches at 5½ n Battalion Front M.29.d.6.0 to M.24.d.2.8½ Land in bad state. Very heavy rain. Nothing to report.	
28th	Situation normal. Progress made in repairs and drainage.	
29th	K. trenches. Situation normal. Relieved by 2.C.G at 5 p.m. Battn. moved to billets at PONT DU HEM	
30th	In billets	
31st	Battn. relieved 2.C.G. in trenches, 8 from honourable marched gun. + rifle fire by enemy throughout night. Not unusual. Influenced by bursts of machine gun + rifle gun & rifle fire for few mins	

J. Campbell
Lieut Colonel
Commanding 3rd Battn Coldstream Guards

1st Guards Brigade.
Guards Division.

3rd BATTALION

COLDSTREAM GUARDS.

JANUARY 1 9 1 6

Army Form C. 2118.

WAR DIARY
or
INTELLIGENCE SUMMARY.
(Erase heading not required.)

Instructions regarding War Diaries and Intelligence Summaries are contained in F.S. Regs., Part II. and the Staff Manual respectively. Title pages will be prepared in manuscript.

3rd BATTN. COLDSTREAM GUARDS

Hour, Date, Place	Summary of Events and Information	Remarks and references to Appendices
Jan 1st 1916. 2nd	In trenches East end of December. All Quiet	
3rd.	All quiet. Enemy snipers less active. Relieved by 2 C.G at 5.0 p.m. To billets at PONT DU HEM.	
4th.	Billets PONT DU HEM. Relieved 2 C.G. Trenches. Quiet night.	
5th.	In trenches. Situation normal.	
6th.	In trenches. Pvt H.C. Lewis killed morning afternoon Relieved at 4.30 p.m. by 4th W. Welsh Regt. PONT DU HEM.	15th ? v Day 1st Welsh Bde.
7th.	Billets. Moved 11.15 a.m. to billets nr ROBECQ.	
8th – 12th.	At billets near ROBECQ	
12th.	Moved to billets at LE SART.	
13th – 26th.	In billets at LE SART.	
25th.	Moved to relieve Scots at PONT DU HEM.	
26th.	Relieved 2 C.G. in trenches (Same line as Decr.) 5 p.m. Quiet night.	
27. – 29. 26.	In trenches. Situation normal. Relieved by 2 C.G.	
29 & 30	5 p.m. 28th.	
	Billets at PONT DU HEM. Relieved 2 C.G. in trenches. 5.0 p.m. 30th.	
31st.	In trenches. Situation normal.	

J. Campbell
Lt. Colonel
Comdg.
3rd Bn. Coldstream Gds.

1st Guards Brigade.
Guards Division.

3rd BATTALION

COLDSTREAM GUARDS.

FEBRUARY 1916

Army Form C. 2118.

WAR DIARY
or
INTELLIGENCE SUMMARY.
(Erase heading not required.)

3rd BATTN. COLDSTREAM GUARDS

Hour, Date, Place	Summary of Events and Information	Remarks and references to Appendices
Feb 1st	In trenches. Situation normal. Relieved by 2 C.G.	
" 2nd + 3rd	In billets PONT DU HEM	
" 3rd	In billets PONT DU HEM	
" 4th + 5th	Relieved 2 C.G. in trenches at 5.30 p.m. All quiet. Ammonal Torpedo Experiments not carried out owing to station being cancelled.	
" 5th	In trenches. Snipers on both sides active.	
" 6th	Relieved by 2 C.G. to billets PONT DU HEM	
" 7th	In billets PONT DU HEM	
" 8th	at billets near MERVILLE 11.15 a.m.	
" 9th — 15th	In billets near MERVILLE	
" 15th	Battn. moved to ST SYLVESTRE	
" 16th	Battn. moved to Camp 2 miles N. of POPERINGHE	
" 16th to 25th	In camp at POPERINGHE	
" 26th	Marched to BAVINCHOVE station. Arrived 6.30 p.m. Entrained for CALAIS. Train depart 5.30 a.m. Arrived CALAIS 6.36 a.m. Marched to No. 6. LARGE REST CAMP	
" 26th to 29th	At Rest Camp at CALAIS	

J. Campbell
Lt Colonel
Comdg
3rd Bn Coldstream Guards

1st Guards Brigade.
Guards Division.

3rd BATTALION

COLDSTREAM GUARDS.

MARCH 1 9 1 6

3 Coldstream Gds.
Vol XIV

Army Form C. 2118.

WAR DIARY
or
INTELLIGENCE SUMMARY.
(Erase heading not required.)   3rd Bn Coldm Guards.

Page 1

Instructions regarding War Diaries and Intelligence Summaries are contained in F. S. Regs., Part II and the Staff Manual respectively. Title pages will be prepared in manuscript.

Hour, Date, Place	Summary of Events and Information	Remarks and references to Appendices
March 1st to 5th	In Camp at CALAIS.	
5th	Moved by train from CALAIS 10.20 pm. to BAVINCHOVE	
6th	Arrived BAVINCHOVE STN. 2-30 am. Detrained marched through snowstorm to Billets at WENEKEN PUT.	
7th to 15th	In Billets at KLIENEN PUT. On 15th moved at 3.0 pm by march route to Camp WEST of POPERINGHE.	
16th	Battn marched at 5.0 pm. to Camp of Huts 2½ miles N.W. of POPERINGHE	
17th	Battn. moved 6.0 pm by train to YPRES thence marched to YSER CANAL BANK.	
18th	Battn. moved at 7.0 pm. and marched to trenches taking over left Sub. Section of Brigade Sector. FROM:- FENCHURCH STREET, C. 29. a. 31. TO:- PRATT STREET, C. 28. a. 48 on left. 2nd Battn. Grenadier Guards on Right, 20th Division on Left.	
19th	Whole line in bad state. Parapets weak etc. No drainage. No communication by day to WIELTJE SALIENT except by HAYMARKET, RIGHT of ODE SECTOR. Fairly quiet day. Some hostile shelling without much damage. Uneventful night. Patrols caught nothing. Coys all hard at work revetting.	
20th	Quiet day. Relieved at 10.0 pm. by 2nd C.G. Battn to CANAL BANK.	
21st to 22nd	CANAL BANK. Very wet.	
22nd	Relieved 2 CG in trenches, same trenches 10.0 pm Quiet night	
23rd	Bad day. WIELTJE SALIENT heavily shelled about 2-afternoon 100 gas shells thrown in and all communications cut. No work possible before dark. During night communication made. SALIENT alarmed & "pare attack" ready. No actual Many attacked. 1 Officer 26 O.R. Morgue.	

(73989) W4141—463. 400,000. 9/14. H.&J.Ltd.   Forms/C. 2118/10.

WAR DIARY
INTELLIGENCE SUMMARY

Army Form C. 2118.

3rd Bn. Coldm. Gds.

Hour, Date, Place	Summary of Events and Information	Remarks and references to Appendices
March 24th	Quiet day. Very little work possible during daytime. All Coy at work at dusk on parapets & drains. Relieved at 10.0 pm by 2 C.G. Batt. to ENNISBANK	
25th	Quiet day along the CANAL	
26th	Moderate day. Some shelling. Relieved 2 C.G. in trenches 9 & 10.	
27th	WHEATIE SALIENT again blown. Relief delayed owing to shell fire. Relief complete 12.45 am. Coy at work repairing but delayed by shell fire. Intermittent hostile shelling during day. Work throughout night carried on. Salient again blown up and built up.	
28th	Fairly quiet morning. Hostile 8 in. again troublesome but damage lessened by strong wind. Relieved by 2 C.G. 10.0 pm. Batt. to CANAL BANK.	
29th	CANAL BANK. Quiet.	
30th	Hostile bombardment throughout day. Relieved 2 C.G. in trenches 10.0 pm. Quiet during relief.	
31st	Enemy very quiet. Very little hostile shelling. Quiet night. All Coys at work on parapets, repairs and drainage.	

J. Campbell.
Lieut Colonel
Commanding
3rd Bn. Coldstream Guards

1st Guards Brigade.
Guards Division.

3rd BATTALION

COLDSTREAM GUARDS.

APRIL 1 9 1 6

Army Form C. 2118.

WAR DIARY
or
INTELLIGENCE SUMMARY. 3rd Bn. Coldstream Gds.

(Erase heading not required.)

Vol 15

Hour, Date, Place	1916	Summary of Events and Information	Remarks and references to Appendices
April	1st	In trenches. Quiet day, enemy machine Relieved by 2 C.G. at 10 pm. Relief carried out under great difficulties and under heavy hostile shell fire which continued throughout the night. Bn. to Canal Bank.	
	2nd.	Quiet day on Canal Bank.	
	3rd.	1st Gds. Bde. relieved by 3rd Gds. Bde. Bn. moved from Canal Bank by train from YPRES to POPERINGHE. In billets.	
	5th to 10th	In billets in POPERINGHE. On 10th Bn. moved about 6 pm to Camp "A" West FLAMERTINGHE for one night.	
	11th	Very wet. At 5 pm Bn. moved by tram to YPRES and marched up to the line and relieved 3rd Bn. Grenadier Gds. (2nd Gds Bde.) taking over LEFT Sub Sector of LEFT Sector of DIVISIONAL Area. Dispositions:- (a) 1 Coy plus 2 Platoons in front line. 2 Platoons J. line. 1 Coy X.3. 2 Platoons Northern End X.2. 2 Platoons I07 I7C defences Quiet night. Trenches very wet and parapets bad. Only one communication trench fit for use, and that not good.	Trench Sheet 28 D.F.O. Rt. of Bn. I.5. B. 1.4. Left " I.5. B. 1.4. 2nd Bn. Grenadier Gds. on right & Bn. 3rd Gds. Bde. on left.
	12th to 15th	Wet weather - bad trenches. Trench routine as usual. All Coys. kept a work throughout on drainage and general renovating of line. Enemy artillery quiet but amount of very hostile Enemy M.G. fire interfered with work. Relieved 9 pm. 15.4. by 2 C.G. Bn. moved by train from YPRES to Camp A.	

Cox
Lt. Col.
Commanding
3rd Bn Coldstream Gds.

(73989) W4141—463. 400,000. 9/14. H.&J.Ltd. Forms/C. 2118/10.

Army Form C. 2118.

WAR DIARY
or
INTELLIGENCE SUMMARY. 3rd Bn. Coldstream Gds.

(Erase heading not required.)

Instructions regarding War Diaries and Intelligence Summaries are contained in F. S. Regs., Part II. and the Staff Manual respectively. Title pages will be prepared in manuscript.

Hour, Date, Place	Summary of Events and Information	Remarks and references to Appendices
April 1916		
16th to 19th	In Camp A. Left Support Bn.	
19th	Bn. relieved 2 C.G. in trenches moving by train to YPRES. Delayed owing to Heavy Hostile Bombardment. Quiet night after relief.	
20th to 23rd	In trenches. Weather very bad. Heavy rain. Trenches awful since after 36 hours ceaseless rain. Work impossible by day. All men available at work by night.	
23rd	A fine day. Floods subsiding. Our snipers claim 1 German. Relieved by 2 C.G. at 9 p.m. Bn. moved back to Camp A.	
24th to 26th	In Camp A.	
27th	Bn. moved 6.30 p.m. to Billets in POPERINGHE.	
28th to 30th	In billets at POPERINGHE.	

J Campbell
Lt. Col.
Comdg.
3rd Bn. Coldstream Guards.

1st Guards Brigade.
Guards Division.
—

3rd BATTALION

COLDSTREAM GUARDS.

MAY 1916

Army Form C. 2118.

WAR DIARY or INTELLIGENCE SUMMARY.

3rd Bn. Coldstream Gds.

(Erase heading not required.)

Hour, Date, Place	Summary of Events and Information	Remarks and references to Appendices
May 1st 6.4.M	In billets in POPERINGHE. Batt. moved 6.30p.m. a 4th by Coys. to Camp B. and relieved 1st Bn. Scots Gds.	
5th	Bn. moved up into the line, by train at dusk and took over Trenches 3rd Grenadier Gds. Right Sub Section of Left Brigade. Quiet night. Relief normal.	
6th	Quiet day. Road heavily shelled by enemy throughout the night.	
7th 8th	In trenches. Situation normal. Very little work possible by day. Progress made at night on wiring of front.	
9th	Situation normal. Batt. relieved by 1st C.G. at 9.30 p.m. On relief Batt. moved by train to Camp B.	
10th to 13th	Camp B. Manual routine. 9th	
13th	Relieved 2 C.G. in trenches 9.30 p.m. Quiet night.	
14th	In trenches. Menin intermittent hostile shelling without much damage. Otherwise normal.	
15th	Enemy attempted to break left of our front line. They were driven off with bombs & Lewis Gun fire, just before daylight. Hostile machine guns very active throughout night 15/15/15. Intermittent shelling both camps. Relieved by 2 C.G. at 10 p.m. Batt. moved by train from YPRES to Camp B. Quiet night.	
17th	Rest in Camp B.	
18th	Bn. marched at 9 a.m. to Camp "L" WEST OF POPERINGHE. Shelled all the way to POPERINGHE.	
19th	Bn. marched at 7.40 a.m. to HOPPOUTRE SIDING and entrained for ST OMER. Arrived 12.20 p.m. Detrained and marched to the Barracks (17th INFANTRY BARRACKS) Whole Bn. in barracks. Officers billetted in Town.	

J. Campbell Lt. Col.
Comdg. Gds.
3rd Bn. Coldm. Gds.

WAR DIARY
or
INTELLIGENCE SUMMARY. 3rd Bn. Coldstream Guards.

Army Form C. 2118.

Hour, Date, Place	Summary of Events and Information	Remarks and references to Appendices
May 20th 31st 1916.	Bn. billetted ST OMER for training. Programme arranged to Progressive training. Work done from 22 to 29th by platoons.	

J. Campbell /
Lt. Col.
Comdg.
3rd Bn. Coldstream Guards.

1st Guards Brigade.
Guards Division.

3rd BATTALION

COLDSTREAM GUARDS.

JUNE 1916

WAR DIARY
INTELLIGENCE SUMMARY. 3rd Bn. Coldstream Gds.

Army Form C. 2118.

(Erase heading not required.)

Hour, Date, Place	Summary of Events and Information	Remarks and references to Appendices
June 1st to 6th	Bn. billetted at ST OMER for training. Work done – June 1 to 3 by Coys. 5 to 6 Battalion.	
7th	Bn. marched 8.30 a.m. to billets at ST MARIE CAPPEL. 1st Gds. Bde. moving up.	
8th	Bn. marched 7.30 a.m. to Camp "N" WEST of POPERINGHE.	
9th to 16th	At Camp "N". 200 men employed daily on Rly. construction. 100 men nightly on dugouts on Canal Bank.	
16th	Bn. moved to YSER CANAL BANK into dugouts on WEST BANK (one Coy EAST). Moved by tram to ASYLUM, YPRES, thence by hand route. (1st Gds. Bde. took over LEFT SECTOR of DIVISIONAL FRONT. MAP REF. TO⁷⁰ ST JULIAN. N.W.2.	
17th to 20th	Canal Bank. Intermittent hostile shelling each day. Right D.22 – Left 35 4 day relief Bn. in left Sub-Sector of Brigade Section, ie left of British line. look over Reserve. Description. Bad line. Parapets too low. Communication not existent by day. 2 Coys in front line, 2 Coys in Support, 2nd Grenadier Gds on our right. French troops on our left, supported by Belgian Artillery. Quiet night. Enemy snipers active from left flank.	
(21st, 22nd, 23)	In trenches. Little work possible by day in front trenches. Very heavy work necessary by night on parapets drainage. Wire & communications.	
24th	In trenches. Our Artillery bombarded enemy positions throughout the day commencing 9.0 a.m.	

J Campbell Lt. Col.
Comdg.
3rd Bn. Coldstream Gds.

WAR DIARY or INTELLIGENCE SUMMARY

Army Form C. 2118.

3rd Bn. Coldstream Gds.

(Erase heading not required.)

Instructions regarding War Diaries and Intelligence Summaries are contained in F.S. Regs., Part II. and the Staff Manual respectively. Title pages will be prepared in manuscript.

Hour, Date, Place 1916.	Summary of Events and Information	Remarks and references to Appendices
June 24th (contd)	Enemy retaliated on our trenches in afternoon. Blown up in several places. Casualties slight. Relieved by 2 Coy. after dark. Bn. withdrawn to Canal Bank into Left Reserve.	
25th	Quiet day. Canal Bank shelled during evening.	
26th	Wet day. Trenches much damaged. 3 Coys. at work day & night on communication trenches. Very bad night for work. Very heavy rain till 2.0 a.m.	
27th	Canal Bank. Our artillery bombarded enemy positions throughout the day. Some retaliation along our front. Casualties slight. Bn. relieved during night by 1st Scots Gds. (3rd Gds. Bde.) & marched to Camp E in A.30.	
28th	Quiet day. Bn. resting, cleaning up. Remainder of 1st Gds. Bde. Camped out during night 28th/29th.	
29th-30th	In Camp E. Coys. at Drill & instruction.	

J. Campbell
Lt. Col.
Comdg.
3rd Bn. Coldstream Guards.

1st Guards Brigade.
Guards Division.

3rd BATTALION

COLDSTREAM GUARDS.

JULY 1916

Vol 78. 1 Gds Bde.

Army Form C. 2118.

WAR DIARY
or
INTELLIGENCE SUMMARY.

(Erase heading not required.)

3rd Bn. Coldstream Gds.

Instructions regarding War Diaries and Intelligence Summaries are contained in F.S. Regs., Part II. and the Staff Manual respectively. Title pages will be prepared in manuscript.

Hour, Date, Place	Summary of Events and Information	Remarks and references to Appendices
July 1916		
1st	Div. Reserve Camp E.	
2nd to 5th	do	
6 H.	Move in evening to relieve 3rd Gds. Bde. Left Reserve Bathurst at CHATEAU TROIS TOURS.	
7 H.	From TROIS TOURS in the evening relieved 2nd Scots Guards. Left Front Bn. Right Bde.	
8 H.	In trenches. Right Front Coy. In HORSE DE MORTELDUE LINE.	
9 H.	" " Right Front Coy very heavily MINNEWHEREFERED	
10 H & 11 H	" "	
12 H.	" " Relieved by 2nd Bn. C.G. proceeded to CHATEAU TROIS TOURS	
13th to 16th	TROIS TOURS.	
16 H.	Relieved 2nd Bn. in trenches.	
17 H & 19 H.	In trenches. Relieved on 19th by 2 C.G.	
20 H. 22nd	TROIS TOURS. Relieved 2nd in trenches on night of 22nd	
22nd to 25th	In trenches. Relieved on night of 25th by 2 C.G. marched to TROIS TOURS.	
26 H.	TROIS TOURS. Relieved Royal Fnsd. Fusiliers. Entrained at YLAMERTINGHE.	
27 H.	Arrived Camp "M". (W. of POPERINGHE). Left Camp M in afternoon marched to HERZEELE.	
28 H.	Billet in HERZEELE.	
29 H.	Left HERZEELE in evening, marched to PROVEN.	
30 H.	Entrained at PROVEN (12 midnight). Detrained ST POL at 6.15 a.m. By bus to Busenecourt BOUQUE MAISON	
31st	Busenecourt BOUQUE MAISON.	

J. Campbell
Lt. Col.
Comdg.
3rd Bn. Coldstream Gds.

(73989) W4141—463. 400,000. 9/14. H.&J.Ltd. Forms/C. 2118/10.

1st Guards Brigade.
Guards Division.

3rd BATTALION

COLDSTREAM GUARDS.

AUGUST 1916

WAR DIARY or INTELLIGENCE SUMMARY

(Erase heading not required.)

Army Form C. 2118.

Vol 19 3rd Bn. Coldstream Gds.

Instructions regarding War Diaries and Intelligence Summaries are contained in F.S. Regs., Part II. and the Staff Manual respectively. Title Pages will be prepared in manuscript.

Place	Date	Hour	Summary of Events and Information	Remarks and references to Appendices
	10th		Marched at 6 a.m. from BOVQUE MAISON to VAUCHELLES, where Bn. Camped in Huts.	
	2nd 9th	10 h.	In Camp at VAUCHELLES. On 9th visited by H.M. The King.	
			C.O. + Coy Comdrs inspected trenches opposite BEAUMONT HAMEL. Bn. marched at 4.45 p.m. to BERTRANCOURT + billeted in Huts in the village.	
	11th		Relieved 9th Bn. Suffolk Regt. in the trenches. Coys marching at 1 hr. intervals from 7.45 a.m. via VITERMONT. — To trenches — Thence positions:- 2 Coys. Front Line. 2 Coys Support. Area Map Ref. (Trench Map France Sheet 57 D. SE 1/20000). Right :- Q.6.B.7.9. (inclusive). Left Q.10.B.2.1. (exclusive). Bn occupied Left Sub Sector of Right Sector of Div. Area. 2nd Bn. Grenadier Gds on Right. 2nd Guards Bde. on Left.	
			Trenches Good + Deep but whole area very dirty + unsanitary. No dugouts in Front Line. Some deep dugouts in Support. Front line slightly held. Relief carried out in Daylight. Completed at 2.45 p.m. Very Slow.	
	12th		Quiet day + night. Quiet day in trenches. Coys at work on improvements + general cleaning. Sewer Coys employed throughout night in gaps in enemy's wire.	
	13th		Quiet. Occasional bursts of hostile shelling. Our aeroplanes very active in this area. Hostile planes seldom come up.	
	14th		Quiet night. Coys at work on shell slits. Relieved by 9th Bn. Norfolk Regt. 71st Bde. Relief complete 1.15 p.m. Bn marched to BERTRANCOURT and occupied Huts.	
	15th		Quiet day. No move.	
	16th		Bn. marched at 3.30 p.m. to COUIN, + occupied Huts. 31st Division + Reserve under direct orders of Division.	
	17-19		In Divisional Reserve at COUIN. Weather Bad.	

J. Campbell
Lt. Col.
Comdg.
3rd Bn. Coldstream Guards.

WAR DIARY or INTELLIGENCE SUMMARY

Army Form C. 2118.

3rd Bn. Coldstream Gds.

Place	Date 1916	Hour	Summary of Events and Information	Remarks and references to Appendices
August	20th		Relieved by 1st Bn. Kings Liverpool Regiment. Bn. marched at 11:0 am to Camp of Huts in WARNIMONT WOOD EAST OF AUTHIE. 1st Gds Bde concentrated	
	21-22		In Camp in WARNIMONT WOOD.	
	23rd		Marched at 9am to Billets at BEUVAL. About 10 miles.	
	24th		Marched at 8am. to Billets at FRESSELLES. 9 miles.	
	25th		Marched at 11.30 am. to CANAPLES. 3 miles. Entrained in Indian train at 2.40 (40 minutes late) railed to MERICOURT L'ABBEY. Arrived at 9.0 pm. after very slow journey. Marched to Billets at MEAULTE, arriving at 11.30 pm.	
	26, 31		In Billets at MEAULTE. Corps at work on General Instruction & fatigues.	

J. Campbell
Lieut Colonel,
Comdg.
Coldstream Guards.
3rd Bn. Coldstream Guards.

1st Brigade.
Guards Division.

3rd BATTALION

COLDSTREAM GUARDS.

SEPTEMBER 1916

Army Form C. 2118

WAR DIARY
or
INTELLIGENCE SUMMARY

(Erase heading not required.) 3rd Bn. Coldstream Guards.

Vol 20

Place	Date 1916	Hour	Summary of Events and Information	Remarks and references to Appendices
	Sept. 1st to 10th		Billets at MEAULTE. On 10th moved at 10 a.m. to bivouacs at CARNOY.	
	11th to 14th		Bivouacs at CARNOY. At 7.50 p.m. 14th moved to Trenches near GINCHY, relieving 2nd Grenadier Guards about midnight. The Bn. took up position for assault. Dispositions: No. 1 Coy. Right Front. No. 2 Coy. Left Front. " 4 " " Support. " 3 " " Support. 2nd Bn. Coldstream Guards on right. N.O.Y.L.I. on left.	
	15th		At 6 a.m. the K.O.Y.L.I. Tank advanced on our left to clear our flank, where the situation was somewhat obscure. At 6.20 a.m. the assault was launched. The Bn. advanced from the 2 Coys. waves at 50 paces interval. The attack was met with great opposition from the Sunken Road about 500 yds from our trenches. After this had been overcome the GREEN line was taken without much opposition. Here the Bn. reorganised, then pushed forward to the BROWN line which the enemy had evacuated. Consolidation was begun. About 6 p.m. the enemy made a counterattack which was easily repulsed. After dark rations, water & ammunition were brought up. Bn. finally consolidating BROWN line. Total casualties Offrs. 11 O.R. 414	
	16th 17th		Relieved at 5 p.m. by Bde. Marched back to CITADEL.	
	18th to 20th		Camp at CITADEL. On 20th the Bn. moved at 7 p.m. relieved 12th K.R.R. 12th K.R.B. in Trenches about T.9 & T.6 of map sheet 57J S.E.	
	21		Relieved 1st Bn. Grenadier Guards about midnight. Bn. Battle Front in Trenches facing LES BOEUFS.	
	22nd to 24th		Bde. Battle Front. Heavy hostile shelling. On 24th relieved about 10 p.m. by 1st Bn. Irish Guards. Bn. took up Support position in main Communication trench. Dispositions: No. 3 Coy. Right Front. Afterwards Capt. " 4 " Left Front Hopwood " 1 " " Support took " 2 " " Support Comdt. Coldstm.	

3rd Bn. Coldstm.

WAR DIARY or INTELLIGENCE SUMMARY

(Erase heading not required.) 3rd Bn. Coldstream Gds.

Army Form C. 2118

Place	Date 1916	Hour	Summary of Events and Information	Remarks and references to Appendices
	Sept. 25th		Bn. moved forward to GREEN line at 1.35 p.m. No.3 Coy. were then sent forward to Bomb through Northern end of LES BOEUFS, when to take up a position in front of LES BOEUFS - GAUDECOURT Road, in support. No.1 Coy. advanced to BROWN line and started to dig in, followed by No.4 Coy, + ½ of No.2. About 4 p.m. No.1 Coy. + ½ of No.2 Coy went forward from the BROWN line and dug in immediately in front of LES BOEUFS, in close support to the Brisk. The remaining half of No.2 Coy were kept at Bn. H.Q. as Reserve.	
	26.		Consolidation of line. Heavy hostile shelling. Relieved about 9 p.m. by Coy of 2nd Irish Guards. Moved to bivouacs at CARNOY. Casualties { 1 Offr. 136 O.R.	
	27		Moved at 7.30 p.m. to Camp at F.13.	
	28		Camp at F.13.	
	29		Moved at 4 p.m. to SANDPITS CAMP.	
	30		" 2.30 " " Billets at MORLANCOURT. Bats. move.	

Bowness Capt.
Comdg.
3rd Bn. Coldstream Gds.

1st Guards Brigade.
Guards Division.

3rd BATTALION

COLDSTREAM GUARDS.

OCTOBER 1916

WAR DIARY or INTELLIGENCE SUMMARY

Army Form C. 2118.

3rd Bn Coldstream Gds

October 1916

Vol 21

Place	Date	Hour	Summary of Events and Information	Remarks and references to Appendices
	1916 Oct 1st		Battalion moved in French Motor lorries from MORLANCOURT to SELINCOURT.	
	Oct 2nd to Oct 31st		Battalion in Billets at SELINCOURT. Battalion on Company Training.	

J. Campbell
Lt. Col.
Comdg.
3rd Bn. Coldstream Guards.

1st Guards Brigade.
Guards Division.

3rd BATTALION

COLDSTREAM GUARDS.

NOVEMBER 1 9 1 6

Army Form C. 2118.

3rd Bn. Coldstream Guards

WAR DIARY
or
INTELLIGENCE SUMMARY

(Erase heading not required.)

November 1916 Vol 22

Instructions regarding War Diaries and Intelligence Summaries are contained in F. S. Regs, Part II. and the Staff Manual respectively. Title Pages will be prepared in manuscript.

Place	Date	Hour	Summary of Events and Information	Remarks and references to Appendices
Selvincourt	Nov 2	1 P	Inspection of Guard Div by H.R.H. Duke of Connaught at Brouement.	
"	2nd - 9th		Billets Selvincourt.	
"	10th		Moved by French Motor Lorries to Citadel Camp. Left 9 a.m. arr. 8½ a.m.	
	11th		Marched to Camp 'A' Trones Wood.	
	12th - 15th		Relieved 7th Yorks Regt & 4th E. Yorks in trenches N. of Les Boeufs and took over line three nights - with 1st Batt. Irish Guards on left and troops of 6th Div on right.	
			Relieved night of 15th by 2nd Batt. Rles Essex Regs and marched back to HW Camp, Trones Wood.	
	16th - 18th		In H.Q. Camp.	
	19th		Moved to Sandpits Camp	
	20th - 26th		In Sandpits Camp	
	27th		Moved to Forked Tree Camp	
	28th - 30th		In Forked Tree Camp.	

W.H. Crawford
Lt Col.
Commg 3rd Batt. Coldstream Guards

1st Guards Brigade.
Guards Division.

3rd BATTALION

COLDSTREAM GUARDS.

DECEMBER 1 9 1 6

WAR DIARY
INTELLIGENCE SUMMARY
(Erase heading not required.)

Army Form C. 2118.

December 1916

3rd Bn. Coldstream Gds.

Vol 23

Place	Date	Hour	Summary of Events and Information	Remarks and references to Appendices
FORKED TREE Camp	1st	—	Preparations for moving up to line	
"	2nd	12 noon	Bn moved to MALTZ HORN FARM CAMP.	
MALTZ. HORN	3rd-5th		Bn relieved 114th Bgt French Infantry. SAILLY-SAILLISEL. C.8.6.2.1. to C.1.6.5.7. - 3rd Bn Grenadier Guards on our left - Frenck 20th Corps on our right.	
Trenches	5th	6 p.m.	Bn relieved by 4 GG and party of 1st Scots Guards and 1 Coy 1st Coldstm Gds. retired to MALZ HORN CAMP.	
MALZ HORN	6th		Moved by train from TROVES WOOD to BROMFAY. CAMP 15.	
BROMFAY	7th		In Camp.	
"	8th		"	
"	9	11.30	Marched to COMBLES area. relieving 2nd Gren Gds.	
COMBLES	10th		Relieved 1st Coldstream Guards — C.8.c.9.3. - C.8.a.5.7. 2nd Gren Gds on right - 3rd Bn Grenadier Gds on our left.	
TRENCHES	11-12th			
"	12th		Relieved 6 p.m. by 2nd Cold'm Gds returned to MALZ HORN F.M. CAMP	
MALZHORN	13th		Moved by train to BROMFAY.	
BROMFAY	14		Camp BROMFAY. 15.	
"	15		Moved by march route to COMBLES relieving 2nd Gren Gds.	

WAR DIARY or INTELLIGENCE SUMMARY

Army Form C. 2118.

(Erase heading not required.)

Instructions regarding War Diaries and Intelligence Summaries are contained in F. S. Regs., Part II and the Staff Manual respectively. Title Pages will be prepared in manuscript.

Place	Date	Hour	Summary of Events and Information	Remarks and references to Appendices
COMBLES	16	—	Relieved 1st Bn Coldstream Guards in trenches O8a9.3 - O8a5.7. 2nd Grens on our right. 2nd Scots Gds on our left.	
Trenches	17th			
	18th		Bombers relieved by 2nd Grenadiers. Trained from TROVES WOOD back to Camp 103. BROUFAY.	
BROUFAY	19th & 20th			
	21		Move by train to TROVES WOOD. Thence march to COURCELETTE. Relieve 2nd Grens &c.	
COMBLES	22nd		Relieved 1st Bdn from front line trenches. O8a93 - O8a57. 2nd Grens on right — 3rd Grens on left.	
Trenches	23		Ordinary Trench	
"	24		Relieved by 2nd Coy 3rd Bn. 3rd Bn. March to TROVES WOOD. Train to BROUFAY 100.	
BROUFAY	25 & 26th		BROUFAY.	
	27th		Moved to COMBLES area. Move into trenches, relieve 1st C.G. 2nd Grens on right. 3rd Grens on our left.	
COMBLES Trenches	28 29 30		Relieved by 2nd Gd mids - return to BROUFAY 100.	
BROUFAY	31		BROUFAY. 108.	

Signed Maurice 3. Trapps

Army Form C. 2118.

WAR DIARY
or
INTELLIGENCE SUMMARY
(Erase heading not required.)

January 1917.
3rd Bn Coldstream Gds.
WN 24

Instructions regarding War Diaries and Intelligence Summaries are contained in F. S. Regs., Part II. and the Staff Manual respectively. Title Pages will be prepared in manuscript.

Place	Date	Hour	Summary of Events and Information	Remarks and references to Appendices
Meaulte	1st		Batt'n marched from BRONFAY FARM to billets in MEAULTE	
"	2nd – 24th		Batt'n in billets at MEAULTE. Drill and training	
BILLON WOOD	25th		Batt'n marched from MEAULTE to Camp (Huts) in BILLON WOOD	
"	26th – 28th		Batt'n in BILLON WOOD camp.	
PRIEZ FARM	29th		Batt'n marched to trenches and dug outs near PRIEZ FARM in immediate support of 3rd Bde.	
"	30th – 31st		In trenches at PRIEZ FARM.	

WM Crawstone Lt Col
Comdg 3rd Batt. Coldstream Gds

WAR DIARY
or
INTELLIGENCE SUMMARY

(Erase heading not required.)

February 1917   Army Form C. 2118.

3rd Bn. Coldstream Gds

Vol 25

Instructions regarding War Diaries and Intelligence Summaries are contained in F. S. Regs., Part II. and the Staff Manual respectively. Title Pages will be prepared in manuscript.

Place	Date	Hour	Summary of Events and Information	Remarks and references to Appendices
PRIEZ. F^m	1st		In close support.	
"	2nd		Relieved by 1st Bn. Irish Gds - marched to Billon Camp 107.	
BILLON.107	3rd–8th (incl)		Rest and training	
"	9th		Marched to camp at MAUREPAS RAVINE.	
MAUREPAS RAVINE TRENCHES	10th 10th 14th	3½ 14½	Relieved 2nd Bn Scots Gds Left sector, FREGICOURT. U 20 c 5.1 – c 20 6.3 – 32 Connecting. S.O.R.W.	Ref. 57c S40 1/20.000
MAUREPAS RAVINE	10th 14th	X R	Relieved by 2nd Welsh Gds, marched to MAUREPAS RAVINE.	
" "	14th	18th	Brigade Reserve	
" "	18th		Relieved 2nd Bn Coldstream Gds on second Left sector.	
TRENCHES	18th	22nd	Casualties 3 Offs wounded 13. O.R.W. 4.O.R killed	
" "	22nd		Relieved by 2nd Bn Colds brown Guards returned to MAUREPAS RAVINE	
MAUREPAS RAVINE	22nd	25½	Brigade Reserve	
"	25½		Marched to BILLON CAMP 107.	
BILLON CAMP	25th	28th	Bn. Reserve.	

J. Longueville Maj
Commdg
3rd Bn. Coldstream

WAR DIARY

March 1917

3rd Battn. Coldstream Guards

INTELLIGENCE SUMMARY

Vol 26

Place	Date	Hour	Summary of Events and Information	Remarks and references to Appendices
BILLON	1st - 12th		Battn in huts, in Div. Reserve. General training.	
FRÉGICOURT	13th - 15th		Relieved 1st Battn Scots Guards, left support. Battn H.Q. + one company at FRÉGICOURT. Two Companies HAIE WOOD. One company COMBLES	
TRENCHES	16th		Relieved 2nd Battn Grenadier Gds. Two Companies in front of SAILLY - SAILLISEL. Two Companies in rear with Battn H.Q. at HESULE. Enemy withdrawing along our front. POLE trench reoccupied during the night.	
"	17th		BULGAR trench and outskirts of village of MESNIL reoccupied during the night.	
FRÉGICOURT	18th - 19th		Cavalry went through our line and reoccupied front = front. Relieved by 2nd Battn Grenadier Gds about 3 p.m. Two Cos HESULE. Two Cos SAILLY - SAILLISEL	
MAUREPAS	20th - 22nd		Battn relieved by 2nd Battn Coldstream Gds. Moved to MAUREPAS at Bivouacs	

WAR DIARY or INTELLIGENCE SUMMARY

Army Form C. 2118.

3rd Batt. Oxf & Bucks L.I.

March 1917

Place	Date	Hour	Summary of Events and Information	Remarks and references to Appendices
MONTAUBAN	23rd–31st		In Hutts at Montauban. Battn. emp. d on Road – & railway-making fatigues.	

M.J. Crawford
Lt Col.
Comd. 3rd Batt. Oxf & Bucks L.I.

Army Form C. 2118.

WAR DIARY 3rd Batt:
or
INTELLIGENCE SUMMARY Chesham Guards - 1 Batt.

(Erase heading not required.)

April 1917.   Vol 27

Instructions regarding War Diaries and Intelligence Summaries are contained in F. S. Regs., Part II. and the Staff Manual respectively. Title Pages will be prepared in manuscript.

Place	Date	Hour	Summary of Events and Information	Remarks and references to Appendices
Montauban	1st April to 5th April		In huts. Batt: employed road-making and railway making.	
	6th April to 16th April		Batt: moved to Camp ½ mile S. of Le Transloy. Employed daily in road and railway fatigues.	
	17th April to 30th April		Batt: moved to huts (Camp 16) Bronfay Farm. Platoon and Company training.	

W.M? Cran Smith Lt. Col.
Comd. 3rd Batt: Chesham Gds.

2449 Wt. W14957/M90 750,000 1/16 J.B.C. & A. Forms/C.2118/12.

Army Form C. 2118.

WAR DIARY
or
INTELLIGENCE SUMMARY

(Erase heading not required.)

May 1917   3rd Bn Coldstream Guards   Vol 28

Place	Date	Hour	Summary of Events and Information	Remarks and references to Appendices
BRONFAY Camp 16.	1st - 7th		Batt. in hutn Camp 16. Platoon & Company Training daily.	
LE TRANSLOY & W.F.	8th - 10th		Batt. in Camp. Working on YTRES railway.	
ROCQUINY	11th - 19th		Batt. in Camp. " " "	
BRONFAY Camp 15.	20th		Batt. in Camp.	
VAUX (on Somme)	21st - 30th		J. White. Batt = Training.	
	31st		Batt. entrain 3 a.m. for Cattel.	

Major Commandant Lt Col.
Comdg. 3rd Batt. Coldstream Gds.

WAR DIARY
INTELLIGENCE SUMMARY.

June 1917.

3rd Batt: Plateau Scouts

Army Form C. 2118.

Place	Date	Hour	Summary of Events and Information	Remarks and references to Appendices
CLAIRMARAIS.	June 1st to 15th		In billets. General Training. Troops travelling at TILQUES.	
	16th		Batt: marched to billets in WINIZEELE.	
	17th		" " PROVEN.	
	18th		" bivouac in wood near DE WIPPE CABARET.	
	19th - 24th		Batt: employed in burying cables.	
	25th		" moved to new bivouacs 1 mile N.E.	
	26th & 27th		" in bivouac. General fatigues.	
	28th		" relieved 3rd Batt: Grenadier Guards in trenches opposite BOESINGHE.	
	29th & 30th		Batt: holding trenches. Casualties to date 7 O.R. wounded.	

W.M.V. Crawford Lt.Col.
C/o 3rd Batt: Plateau Scouts

July 1917

/G 3rd Bn: Celebrees

Vol 30

Army Form C. 2118.

WAR DIARY
or
INTELLIGENCE SUMMARY.
(Erase heading not required)

Instructions regarding War Diaries and Intelligence Summaries are contained in F. S. Regs., Part II. and the Staff Manual respectively. Title pages will be prepared in manuscript.

Place	Date	Hour	Summary of Events and Information	Remarks and references to Appendices
TRENCHES GOESMIGNE	1.7.17		In the front line in front of ROESINGHE - 38th Div on our right Belgians on our left. Quiet day.	
"	2.7.17		Reft. quiet day	
			Relieved about 10 p.m. by 2nd Bn. Gren Gds. return to CARDOEN Fm. Reached the camp lines ≈ D.R.1.R.10.W.	
CARDOEN FM	3.7.17 – 7.7.17		The Bn. rested at CARDOEN Fm. Enemy found about 100 mens for fatigue every night. Occasional shelling causalities 2 O.R. 2.R. and 19 W.	
	7.7.17		The Bn. relieved Nth Bn. Irish Guards in X-Line (Queen 4) BOESINGHE sector. Quiet day.	
TRENCHES X line BOESINGHE SECTOR	8 – 10.7.17		Fairly quiet time. Capt T.I.K. Devendish killed & 2 n.c.o's wounded.	
	11.7.17		Relieved by 2nd Bn. Gren Gds 11 p.m. then to bivouac at ROUSSIE Tml. Causalties during tour 1 off. K. 1 W. O.R.S.W.	
ROUSSIE Bm.	12.7.17		13th in Reserve to force holding AOR counter attack.	
	13.7.17		13th in Bn. moved to SOUVAUR swing chain when to PROVEN ward the mill & harness.	
PROVEN	15	11.30 am	Bn. moved to billets at HERZEELE – arriving midday	
HERZEELE	16-24		Bn. at billets practising attack on model out ground. Bombing and musketry.	

WAR DIARY
or
INTELLIGENCE SUMMARY.

Army Form C. 2118.

Place	Date	Hour	Summary of Events and Information	Remarks and references to Appendices
HAZZEL	24th		The Bn entrained at 11.30am and were taken to PROVEN and then marched to camp A.4.C.	
A.4.C.	25th		Bn in billets resting well	
A.4.C.	26th		The Bn relieved 2nd Bn Scots Guards and 3rd Bn Gren Guards in BOESINGHE sector. Relief by daylight. Relief being completed by 7pm. 3 N.C.Os on patrol in night.	
TRENCHES BOESINGHE SECTOR	27th		At 11am in preparation was received that there was to be a general attack on the Canal at 11pm. The Bn was ordered to take over S.E. corner BR.W/42 to SOP Bail F.M. & ROCKING Trench with Bn HQrs at CANAL AVENUE and with the attacking Bns... [illegible] ... 3 KBR killed.	
	28th		Bn was relieved at about 5 K15th Scots Guards, and 2nd D.G. and marched to CANON FARM where proceeded by train [?] to CANADA [?]	
	29th		Bn moved to forming up ... 11pm Bn reached forming up area preparing for attack.	
FOREST AREA	30th		... 7 wounded. O.R. 29 K.	
TRENCHES	31st		6am the Bn marched to R.E.F. & M. line in rear Battn Canadian. 10th Bn had O.R. 3 missing.	

F. Jay Lieut Major

3rd Batt. Coldstream Gds.

WAR DIARY or INTELLIGENCE SUMMARY
(Erase heading not required.)

Army Form C. 2118.

Aug 1917.

Vol 31

Place	Date	Hour	Summary of Events and Information	Remarks and references to Appendices
TRENCHES	1.8.17		Batt: relieved 4th Batt: Grenadier Gds in Support line in front of PAULES FARM. Front line on left. 1st Batt: Front guards on right. Casualties. Soldiers rank wounded 1	
"	2.8.17		Batt: relieved 2nd Batt: Scots Guards in Front line, near the STEENBECK. Front line on left. 1st Batt: Front guards on right. Canadian Soldiers rank 14 other rank W	
	3.8.17		Batt: relieved by 2nd Batt: Irish Guards. Casualties 9 other ranks wounded	
	4.8.17		Batt: entrained by tram at 4 a.m. to neighbourhood of PROVEN & occupied camps and huts at PADDOCK WOOD	
PADDOCK WOOD	5.8.17 to 28.8.17		Batt: remained at PADDOCK WOOD. Platoon By Battalion training	
CAMP	29.8.17		Batt: moved by tram to ELVERDINGHE & occupied Bivouacs at CHARTER HOUSE CAMP	
	30.8.17		Batt: finding fatigue parties on roads & Casualties 3 other ranks and R. 17 other rank wounded	
	31.8.17		Batt: finding fatigue parties on roads Casualties nil	

W.M. Crawford
Lt. Col.
3rd Batt. Coldstream

WAR DIARY
or
INTELLIGENCE SUMMARY.

(Erase heading not required.)

Army Form C. 2118.

September 1919

2nd Bn Rifle Brigade

VM 32

Place	Date	Hour	Summary of Events and Information	Remarks and references to Appendices
CHARTERHOUSE CAMP	1st-8th		The Battn found fatigue parties in forward area. (Casualties Officer 2 wounded extra medical offr OR 2 killed 8 wounded)	
TRENCHES	8th to 12th		The Battn relieved 2nd Battn GCL Rum Guards in WIDYENBUSH sector. 2nd Bn Grenadier Guards on our right. 201st Inf. Regt. on our left. The enemy raided our advanced posts on night of 9/10th and again on 11/12th but was repulsed. The Battn was relieved by 2nd Bn KRR Guards and returned to V Sector. Casualties during this tour 1 Officer killed OR 12 killed & wounded 3 missing.	
HEWLEY CAMP	13th to 20th		From LUMAVILLE Fm to 15th HEWLEY CAMP. In Camp	
PADDOCK WOOD	20th		The Bn moved to PADDOCK WOOD CAMP	
PADDOCK WOOD	20th to 30th		Platoon training. Platoon practising attack. Lectures etc. 2 Coys went to CAMBRIDGE CAMP from 25th-27th. According to the R.S.B. Casualties for week attd.	

W.J. Crosspond Lt.M.
Comd 2nd Bn Rifle Brigade

WAR DIARY or INTELLIGENCE SUMMARY

Army Form C. 2118.

October 1917.

2nd BN. COLDSTREAM GUARDS

Place	Date	Hour	Summary of Events and Information	Remarks and references to Appendices
NORTHERN CAMP			The Battn. was in camp from Oct 1 to the 7th inst. Training.	
PADDOCK WOOD CAMP	Oct 7		Battn. moved by train Oct 7th to ETON CAMP. Details and drafts from Bingham L.S.O. went back to Guards Reinforcement Battn. at HERZEELE.	
	Oct 7			
	Oct 9		The Battn. started to take part in the attack from the BROEMBEKE to HOUTHULST FORREST 2 a.m. 5.20 a.m. the Battn. was in support to the 1/4 Battn of the Brigade and passed through the 2nd Battn. C. Gds at the 2nd objective. Final objective was reached at 2 T. 4.40 a distance of 300 yards from the 2nd objective. Battn. HQrs were at EGYPT HOUSE at 6.30 p.m. the 1st Bn. Irish Gds who were on the right contestation ??? some time to ???? to ??? the right and 1 platoon was ??? of our ???? C.O. to form a defensive flank.	
	Oct 10		sat down a number of ??? which was ??? about eventually the night. There were only no casualties during the whole attack. 36 German Prisoners. Battn. was relieved at 8 pm by 103 ??? + 1st/3rd 4th Australian and returned to Louverval in Wood 15.	

Army Form C. 2118.

WAR DIARY
or
INTELLIGENCE SUMMARY.
(Erase heading not required.)

Instructions regarding War Diaries and Intelligence Summaries are contained in F. S. Regs., Part II. and the Staff Manual respectively. Title pages will be prepared in manuscript.

Place	Date	Hour	Summary of Events and Information	Remarks and references to Appendices
	Oct.11		Casualties were 35 O.Rs. killed and 6 Officers killed, 130 O.Rs wounded & no Officers wounded	
			Battalion remained in bivouac from Oct 11 – 16th	
	Oct.14 – 15		Lt Col Crawfurd left for England. (Major Longueville 3rd Dragoon Guards) commanding Brigade again in the line	
	16		Battn. on fatigues	
	18		Battn. entrained at ACQUINGHEM and travelled to PETWORTH Camp (PROVEN a.2)	
	20		Battn. moved by Train to WATTEN & marched 6 miles to NORTBEULINGHEM	
	25		H.R.H Duke of Connaught visited the Battn. at 2.30 p.m.	
To 31st			The C in C reviewed the Division	
28			Training. Though much interfered with by bad weather. From cases of measles permitted in the Battn are being isolated. Isolation lasted for 48 hours only as no fresh cases developed.	

R. Bingham Major
P.S.O.? 3rd Bn., Coldstream Guards

Narrative of Operations from Nov. 27th 6 p.m.
to Dec 5th.

3rd. Bn: Coldstream Guards.

DOIGNIES

Nov. 23rd. At 6pm verbal orders received for the Battn. to parade for the trenches. The Battn. followed the 1st. Bn. Irish Guards and marched via GRAINECOURT to the trenches before FONTAINE NOTRE DAMES relieving the 6th S.H. Relief complete at 5.30 am. No casualties. Comparatively quiet time in the trenches. During the night of the

Nov. 24th. 24th we had to form a defensive flank so as to conform to certain movements of troops on the left but the Battn. front was restored before morning.

Nov. 26th. The Battn. was relieved by the 3rd. Bn. G. Gds. and withdrew to billets in the HINDENBURGH SUPPORT line near RIBECOURT.

Nov. 28th. The Battn. was relieved by the 176th Brigade and marched to billets in METZ EN COUTURE.

Nov. 29th. General swabbing.

Nov. 30th. The Battn. in conjunction with the 2nd. Bn. C. Gds. and the 1st. Bn. Irish Gds. counter attacked the enemy and retook GOUZEAUCOURT. A line was consolidated on the far side of the village.

Dec 1st. Orders were received at 2 am. for the Battn. to attack the QUENTIN RIDGE in conjunction with the 2nd. Bn. G. Gds. on the right and the 3rd. Gds. Bde. on the left. The attack was successful, largely through the gallant behaviour of the Tanks - 4 of which were attached to the Battn. They got into position a few minutes before zero and little could be given them in the way of information as to the objective. Officers who took part in the attack say that it is doubtful if the Battn. would have reached its objective with enough men to consolidate had it not been for the Tanks.
The Battn. was relieved during the night of Dec 1st. and 2nd. by the 1st. Bn. S. Gds.

Dec 2nd. Battn. in billets in sunken road at QUEEN'S CROSS and GOUZEAUCOURT WOOD.

Dec 3rd. The Brigade relieved the 3rd. Gds. Bde. in the line but the Battn. remained in its present quarters.

Dec 4th. The Battn. relieved the 2nd. Bn. C. Gds. in the trenches for 24 hours.

Dec 5th. The Battn. was relieved by the 7th S.H and withdrew to accommodation in GOUZEAUCOURT WOOD.

Dec 6th. The whole Brigade entrained at ETRICOURT and detrained at BEAUMETZ. the Battn. marching to billets at BERNEVILLE.

Casualties for the period Nov 24th to Dec 5th are as under.

Officers	K.	W.	M.	O.R.	K.	W.	M.
Nov. 24		2			2	4	
25					1	13	
26					2	6	
30		9			6	83	3
Dec 1	3	2			9	100	8
5		1				6	
Officers	3	14		O.R.	20	212	11

F. Longueville Lt Col
3rd B? Cold m Guards

3'rd Br Coldstream Guards
November 1917
WK 34

WAR DIARY
or
INTELLIGENCE SUMMARY.
(Erase heading not required.)

Army Form C. 2118.

Place	Date	Hour	Summary of Events and Information	Remarks and references to Appendices
NORTLEULINGHEM	Nov 1/it		Rest & Training.	
	Nov 11		Marched to ENGUINEGATTE } Hazebrouck Sheet 5A	
	Nov 12		" " FIEFS }	
	Nov 13		" " FREVILLERS } Lens Sheet.	
	Nov 17		" " LIENCOURT "	
	Nov 18		" " BLAIREVILLE "	
	Nov 19		" " GOMIECOURT "	
	Nov 22		Moved by bus to BARASTRE area	
	Nov 23		Marched to DOIGNIES arriving 10 a.m. Left DOIGNIES at 6 p.m. and went into the trenches opposite FONTAINE NOTRE DAMES. Battalion relieved 6th S.H. The 119th Inf Bde was on the left. Casualties 2 offrs w. O.R. 5 k. 23 w.	
	Nov 26		Relieved by the 3rd Bn. G. Gds. and withdrew to HINDENBURGH SPT. at RIBECOURT.	
	Nov 28		Relieved by 5th N. Staff (176th Inf. Bde) and marched to METZ EN COUTURE.	
	Nov 29		General assembling of kits.	
	Nov 30		Battn. took part in the Brigade counter attack on GOUZEAUCOURT. Casualties 9 offrs. w. 6 O.R. k. 83 w. 3 m.	
			Officers casualties.	
			2nd Lt. CHALLONER ELDRED CURWEN	3rd Capt. B. Parker-Bowyer 2/Lt. E. Enoch
			Captain DAVID VERNON SHAW KENNEDY (attached)	20. R. H. C. Grant " A. E. Rothwell
	Nov 23			Capt. W. H. B. Pitcher M.C.
				2 R. R. M. Tabuteau
				" H. G. Rickatson
				" A. D. Pyke

J. Campbell Lt. Col.
3rd Bn Coldstream Guards

Army Form C. 2118.

WAR DIARY
or
INTELLIGENCE SUMMARY.
(Erase heading not required.)

Place	Date	Hour	Summary of Events and Information	Remarks and references to Appendices
	6		[illegible handwriting]	
	6		[illegible handwriting]	

3rd Battalion Gds

January, 1918.

Bn went to 31st Division Feby 8"/9/18
4 Gds Bde
Returned to Gds Div. Nov 1918.

WAR DIARY or INTELLIGENCE SUMMARY

2nd Bn Coldstream Guards

January 1918

Army Form C. 2118.

VII 36

Place	Date	Hour	Summary of Events and Information	Remarks and references to Appendices
BERNEVILLE	1.1.18		The Batt'n in billets in the farms in the village	
	2.1.18	9.45am	The Batt'n marched into billets at ARRAS. The whole Bn being billeted in the ECOLE COMMUNAL.	
ARRAS.	2nd – 9.1.18		The Batt'n did chief musketry bombing training. Various ranges were available during this period	
PUDDING TRENCH	10.1.18		The Batt'n relieved 2nd Bn Irish Guards in PUDDING TRENCH (FAUBOUR).	
	10"-14"		The Batt'n found fatigue parties at night	
	14"		Relieved 2nd Bn Coldstream Guards in the sector from The SCARPE to the SOUAI RLY. 1st Bn IRISH GUARDS on our right 3rd Guards Bde on our left.	
Trenches–	14"–18"		There came and left the trenches while in. Enemy threw some TM bombs except in nightly working parties causing minimal casualties. Total Casualties 10ff. Capt MP Stime. W. (at duty). OR. K in A 2. W in A 2. (at duty) W in A 39. OR. K in A 2. W in A 32 (2 at duty 5 dug by) Otherwise very quiet.	
	18"		Relieved by 2nd Bn Coldstream Guards return to PUDDING TRENCH	
			1 Coy near FEUCHY.	
Trenches	18"-21		PUDDING TR. fatigues every night. 20 casualties.	
	22–26		Relies 1st Bn Coldm Gds in front line. 3. O.R. with Bn Coy were Snipt. Casualties	
	26"		Relieved by 1st Bn Scots Guards return to ARRAS. & ECOLE COMMUNAL.	
ARRAS.	26"–31.		Bn remained all Rest Jan. F Lascelles Lt Col. Cmdg 2nd Bn Colstream Guards.	

3/6

On loan from 4" Gds Bde 17/4/18

3rd Coldstream Guards

November
1915

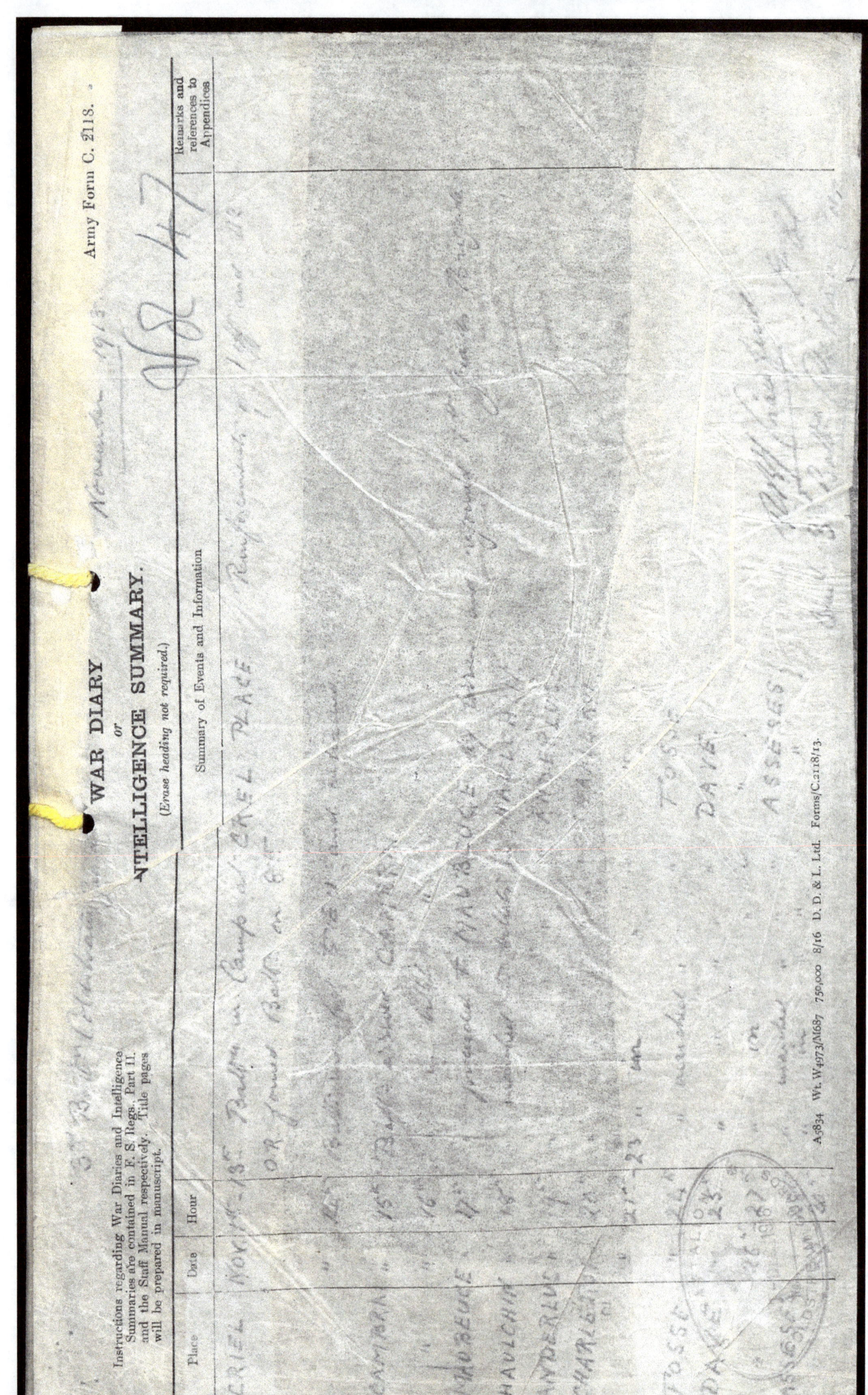

3rd Batt:
Coldstream Guards

WAR DIARY
or
INTELLIGENCE SUMMARY.
(Erase heading not required.)

Army Form C. 2118.

December 1918.

Place	Date	Hour	Summary of Events and Information	Remarks and references to Appendices
ASSESSE	1–4th		Batt: in billets.	
MIECRET.	5th		Batt: marched to new billets.	
BOMAL.	6th		Batt: marched to new billets.	
JEVIGNY.	7th		Batt: marched to billets.	
"	8–10th		Batt: in billets.	
PETIT THIER	11th		Batt: marched to new billets.	
MÖDDERSHEID	12th		Batt: crossed the German frontier at 9.30 a.m. & marched to new billets.	
UNDENBRETH.	13th		Batt: marched to new billets.	
SOTENICH	14th		Batt: marched to new billets. (19 miles)	
KAMMERN	15th		Batt: marched to new billets.	
ERP.	16th		Batt: marched to new billets.	
EPFFEREN	17th		Batt: marched to new billets.	
BICKENDORF	18th–31st		Batt: arrived in billets in suburb of Cologne and was billetted. Large scheme of demobilization of Miners & Battn: being presently re-start by demobilization of Pioneers & "Pivotal" men.	
(cologne)				Com: Bt Guards Bde in Bn

WAR DIARY or INTELLIGENCE SUMMARY.
(Erase heading not required.)

3rd Bn. Coldstream Guards
January–1919.
Army Form C. 2118.

Place	Date	Hour	Summary of Events and Information	Remarks and references to Appendices
Cologne	Jan 1st to Jan 31st		Bn. M. billeted in Cöln Ehrenfeld, a suburb to N. of Cologne. Employed daily in guard mounting – fatigues – route marching – drill & demonstration preceding & to G.O.C. About 200 Pivotal Demobilizers & temp-men were despatched during the week.	

W.H. Crawford
Lt. Col.
Cmd 3rd Bn Coldm Gds

Army Form C. 2118.

WAR DIARY
or
INTELLIGENCE SUMMARY.

February 1919. 3rd Batt. Coldstream Guards

(Erase heading not required.)

Place	Date	Hour	Summary of Events and Information	Remarks and references to Appendices
Cologne	Feb 1st — Feb 28th		The Batt. was billetted in the suburb of Rodenkirchen (Südenorp) and carried on good routine duty. On Feb 18th the 1st (R) Batt'n Coldm Gds. took over from us at Rodenkirchen and the Batt'n became the Reserve Batt'n for that date. No written accounts of events of Feb 1919 retained.	Vol 50

M.V. Crawford Lt. Col.
Comd 3rd Batt Coldstream Gds.

www.ingramcontent.com/pod-product-compliance
Lightning Source LLC
Chambersburg PA
CBHW051528190426

43193CB00045BA/2379